Handmade
Quick Parchment Greetings Cards

Janet Wilson

SEARCH PRESS

First published in Great Britain 2005

Search Press Limited
Wellwood, North Farm Road,
Tunbridge Wells, Kent TN2 3DR

Text copyright © Janet Wilson 2005

Photographs by Roddy Paine Photographic Studios

Photographs and design copyright © Search Press Ltd. 2005

ISBN 1 84448 056 9

The Publishers and author can accept no responsibility for any
consequences arising from the information, advice or
instructions given in this publication.

Suppliers
If you have difficulty in obtaining any of the materials and
equipment mentioned in this book, then please visit the
Search Press website for details of suppliers:
www.searchpress.com

Alternatively, you can write to the Publishers at the address
above, for a current list of stockists, including firms who
operate a mail-order service.

Publishers' note

All the step-by-step photographs in this book feature the
author, Janet Wilson, demonstrating how to make quick
parchment greetings cards. No models have been used.

Manufactured by Universal Graphics Pte Ltd, Singapore

Printed in Malaysia by Times Offset (M) Sdn Bhd

For Michele and Linda

ACKNOWLEDGEMENTS
With many thanks to:
Applicraft UK
Fiskars UK Limited
Letraset Limited, UK
Ranger Industries, USA
Personal Impressions, UK
Post-It Products

Cover
Snowflakes
*The smallest snowflake on the stencil has been used here to
create a veritable flurry of snow!*

Page 1
Two Hearts That Beat As One
*A card for Valentine's Day or, with a different coloured
background, for a wedding.*

Opposite
Jade Bonnet
*The bonnet is coloured with pencils and mounted on to vellum
and card of a similar hue.*

Contents

Introduction

The cards in this book feature a cross between simple embossing techniques and paper pricking borrowed from the original, more time-consuming parchment art form. This book looks at making parchment cards using a basic kit and three-step stencils and suggests ways of mounting your finished pieces as attractive cards. You will learn how to colour the parchment paper prior to embossing as well as how to spot colour areas of the embossed project, using permanent marker pens and coloured pencils. Ideas for freehand decoration of the projects are shown, and how you can devise your own designs by using only parts of the stencils.

For the more adventurous, I suggest more advanced ways of using the stencils, and introduce a couple of basic decorative techniques from the original parchment art form.

If you enjoy all the projects and really get hooked, perhaps you will want to go further and try your hand at the original, ancient art of making parchment cards. In the meantime, enjoy using these simple techniques to make beautiful handmade cards.

Opposite
A selection of cards showing the many different ways the stencils can be used. Embossing, pricking and colouring are combined with decorative techniques borrowed from the original parchment art form.

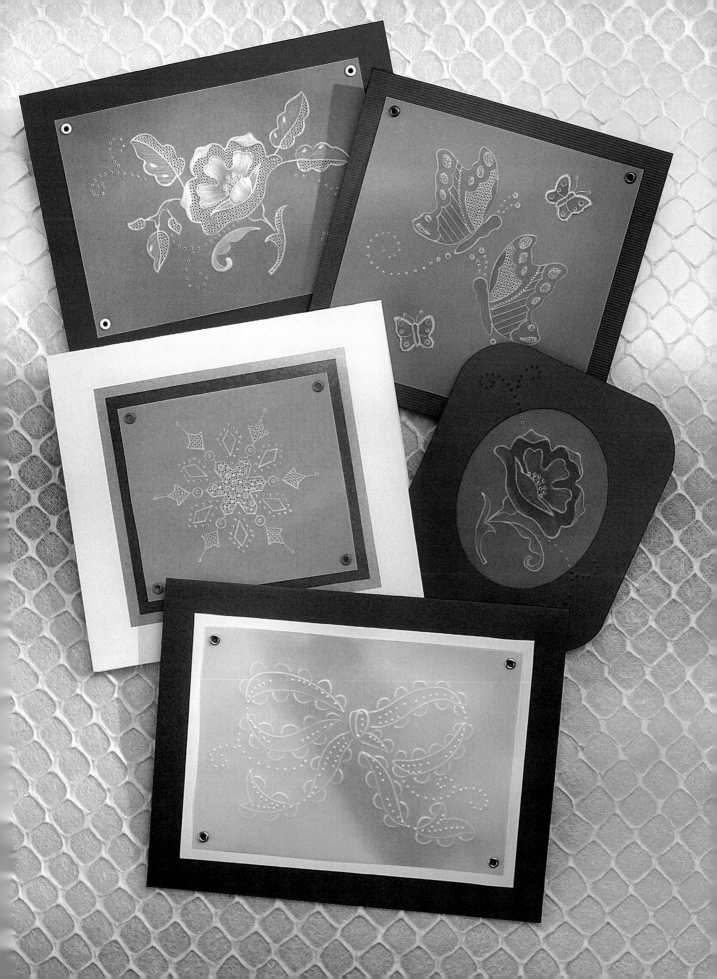

Materials

The basic kit

All the cards in this book were made using a kit produced by Fiskars, plus a few other items. The kit includes:

Mini Shapeboss base This is used in conjunction with duo embossing stencils, meaning that you do not need a light box. The parchamoré system described below has been created to fit this base.

Parchamoré crafting system comprising:

Two sets of three-step stencils, the bow and the rose These are numbered stencils used in order for embossing and perforating designs.

Dual-tip large ball embossing and perforating tool For embossing and perforating areas of the work.

Combined perforating and embossing mat This fits on to the Mini Shapeboss base.

White pencil Used to colour areas of the designs as desired.

160gsm parchment paper I find this too thick and prefer to use a normal weight parchment, which gives a better finish.

Cards and envelopes These are included in the kit so that you can complete projects without having to buy additional materials.

The three-step stencils are numbered 1/3, 2/3 and 3/3 so that you emboss and paper prick the design in the correct order.

Other essentials

Dual-tip medium/small ball embossing tool I prefer to use the medium ball tool rather than the large one that comes with the kit as it produces a more delicate line.

Additional stencils As well as those in the kit, I have used Bonnet, Snowflake, Hearts and Butterfly three-step stencils.

140gsm parchment paper This has been used throughout the book. The maximum width of parchment that can be used on the Mini Shapeboss base is 16cm (6¼in).

A5 piece of 3mm deep fun foam This is used as a mat with the Puerto Rican cutting tools. It can also be used as a perforating mat if you do not want to keep taking the combined mat off the base.

Low tack tape Used to attach the parchment to the combined mat to keep it in place when changing stencils.

Double-sided tape Used to attach layers of paper or card to the base card. Do not use it for attaching parchment, as it will show.

The parchamoré crafting system with the Mini Shapeboss base and additional stencils.

Permanent spray adhesive This can also be used for attaching paper or card to the base card. Do not use it to attach parchment.

Beeswax block Sometimes the embossing tool does not move smoothly over the parchment. Rubbing it across the surface of a beeswax block (or the greasy patch on your chin!) makes it glide easily.

Plastic cutting ruler with a grid Mine has a 0.5cm (³/₁₆in) grid. This makes cutting borders around layers easier.

Craft knife and cutting mat For cutting parchment, paper and card.

Optionals

South American style hard embossing mat This mat really improves your embossing and is essential if you want to use an estralina tool.

Large and small Brazilian estralina This tool was originally used only in Southern Brazil and was a mini drillhead pushed into a mechanical pencil. After my Brazilian colleague and I introduced it to the rest of the world, several companies have brought out their own versions with names such as 'star' or 'sun tool'.

Puerto Rican cutting tools I discovered these in 1986 when I started learning parchment art. Use them on a fun foam mat, just piercing the surface rather than pushing them right down. I have used a medium scallop and straight edge tool in the projects.

Masking tape Used for making the home-made perforating grid (see page 9) and for securing parchment to the grid.

Medium circle hand punch Used for punching holes for eyelets.

Circle aperture cutter Used for making aperture cards into which parchment projects can be mounted.

Corner rounder scissors These are the easiest way to make rounded corners on cards or layers.

Craft punches I have used a snowflake punch and various styles of photo corner punch.

Index tabs These are low tack tabs with a coloured end, ideal for keeping stencils or projects in place.

Mini clips These ultra-mini bulldog clips are wonderful for holding pieces of paper together, (e.g. a pattern with card or parchment) while you cut a piece to size.

Tweezers Useful for picking up eyelets and small punched shapes.

Super non-spray adhesive This tape is excellent for attaching punched shapes to projects. Place the shape on to the sticky side, which is covered with tiny glue dots. Roll the tape back, unroll it, peel off the shape and attach.

Clockwise from the top: Puerto Rican scallop and straight edge cutting tools, craft knife, cutting mat, rulers, spray adhesive, masking tape, fun foam mat, hard embossing mat, brass mesh perforating grid (see page 9), strong scissors, medium circle hand punch (lavender handles), aperture cutter, corner rounder scissors, photo corner punch, star and snowflake punches, beeswax block, index tabs, mini clips, tweezers, small and large estralina tools. Centre: double-sided tape, low tack tape (green in middle) and super non-spray adhesive.

Embellishments

Permanent markers These dry quickly on parchment and the ones I used are available in pastel colours, ideal for parchment projects.

Paint brush Use a flat brush to blend dark and pale shades of permanent marker colours.

Good quality coloured pencils and a blender pencil Artist quality pencils are softer, well pigmented and last a long time. Some ranges are available as individual pencils. A blender pencil is used to blend colours for a professional finish.

Plastic eraser If you have put too much coloured pencil on your work, or gone over the edges, use this before the blender pencil.

Eyelet kit All adhesives show on parchment, and using eyelets is a decorative way to attach projects to layers and/or the base card. The hammer I use has a piercing tool inside the handle, and a setting tool inside that. The piercing tool must never be used with the setting tool inside, or the screw threads will be damaged. Use a setting mat when setting eyelets, as the tool will damage a cutting mat.

Dye inkpads The ink from these can be applied to the back of parchment using a cosmetic sponge, and dries quickly.

Appliqué glue Available in many colours and in metallic or glitter effects. Allow it to dry for at least thirty minutes.

Metallic embroidery thread Used to sew parchment projects to layers or the base card. Use the thread that is sold on bobbins, which comes in many metallic as well as hologram colours.

Beads Use these with metallic thread to add chic to projects.

Clockwise from the top: permanent marker pens, paint brush, appliqué glue, cosmetic sponges, dye inkpads, plastic eraser, blender pencil, eraser pencil, coloured pencils, eyelet setting mat, hammer plus two setting tools, gold thread, cotton bud. Centre: eyelets in various colours and gold beads.

Card and paper

Darker colours work best behind parchment projects. These can then be mounted on to paler coloured card. All adhesives show on parchment, so mount your work using photo corner punches or eyelets.

Paper, card and vellum can all be used to create beautiful cards using quick parchment techniques.

Home-made perforating grid

The perforating grid is used for Argentinian decorative perforating techniques featured in some of the projects where a regular pattern is required. You can make your own using brass mesh and masking tape.

You will need

Brass mesh, gauge 7 holes per cm (³⁄₈in)

Masking tape 2.5cm (1in) wide

Large 6mm (¼in) single hole punch

Black permanent marker

Mat from the parchamoré system

Ruler

Strong scissors

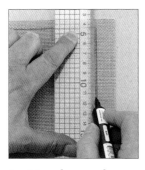
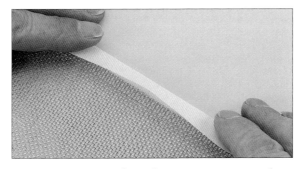

1. Use the marker to draw a rectangle 12 x 16cm (4¾ x 6¼in) on the brass mesh. Cut it out using the strong scissors.

2. Place a piece of masking tape on one of the long sides of the mesh so that the straight edge of the tape is on the third line from the edge of the mesh. Fold the tape in half and position the other edge in alignment with the piece on the front.

3. Repeat this for the other long side and trim any excess masking tape from the ends.

4. On one of the short sides of the mesh, place a piece of masking tape on the third line from the edge of the mesh and stick a second piece of tape exactly behind it. Repeat for the other short side.

5. Place the mat from the parchamoré crafting system on to the mesh and mark where the holes are on the short taped sides.

6. Punch through the tape with the single hole punch to make the holes.

7. The perforating grid now fits on to the Mini Shapeboss base. Place the project on the grid, secure with masking tape and use the perforating tool vertically to perforate through the holes in the relevant areas of the project.

Basic techniques

Making a control piece

The stencils used throughout the book are three-step stencils, two of which are normally for embossing. The third may have a combination of further embossing and perforating work, or may be solely for perforating. I recommend that you make what I call a control piece for each of the sets of stencils you purchase and keep it with the stencils. The control piece shows all the embossing and perforating areas contained on the three-step stencils. When you have made it, you can decide which lines you need not emboss for your project and which parts of the perforating you want to use or leave out. This piece is also of great assistance when you want to change the direction of, say, a piece of ribbon when you start experimenting with more advanced projects using the stencils.

This demonstration shows you how to make a control piece using the bow stencils.

You will need

Basic kit plus Bow three-step stencil

Parchment paper 14.5 x 9.8cm (5¾ x 3⅞in)

Low tack tape

Dual-tip medium/small ball embossing tool

South American style hard embossing mat

Ruler with a grid

Dye inkpads and cosmetic sponges

Scrap card

Permanent markers

Flat no. 4 paint brush

Coloured pencils and blender pencil

Plastic eraser

Large estralina

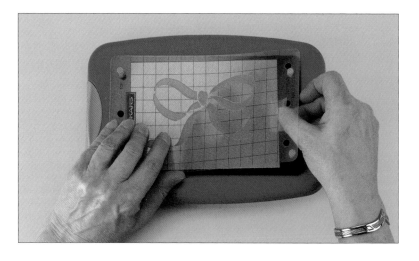

1. Position a piece of parchment underneath stencil 1 and tape it to the mat using low tack tape. You can turn the base when embossing or perforating so that it is in the best position for you.

Tip

If you are using normal weight parchment, you do not have to press hard when embossing. Apply a similar pressure to that which you would use with a pencil.

2. Emboss the areas on stencil 1 using the medium embossing tool. Plastic stencils are prone to move while you are working, so keep your fingers on the stencil to hold it still.

 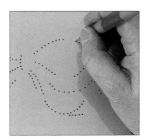 

3. Emboss the areas on stencil 2 in the same way.

4. Perforate with stencil 3 using the perforating tool. Always keep the tool upright when perforating.

The finished control piece. Keep this with the three-step stencils so that you can see at a glance what effects are produced by all the stencils.

Tip

When using the perforating tool, you only need to break the surface of the paper. If you push the tool down too far it will 'bruise' the parchment, leaving a white mark, and you will also distort the hole on the stencil.

Stippling and using white pencil

Normally the control piece would be kept for a reference, but here I have decorated it in order to demonstrate two further techniques.

  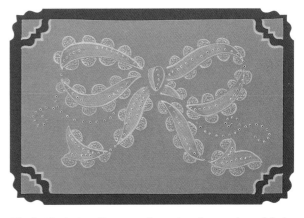

1. Put the parchment on the hard embossing mat or a cutting mat and using the perforating tool, stipple the half-moons along the ribbon edge. Gently bounce the tool up and down.

2. Turn the parchment over and using a white pencil, shade the ribbon area. This will give the design light.

The finished piece. To mount the project, I cut a piece of dark paper measuring 6mm (¼in) more all round than the parchment. A photo corner punch was used on each corner and the parchment was slipped in and secured using small pieces of sticky tape on the back. Spray adhesive or double-sided tape could be used to adhere this layer to the base card.

Cross hatching

This method of decorating parchment projects is used in South America. It is easy to do and the resulting pattern can be decorated in various ways. I recommend using a hard embossing mat for this work.

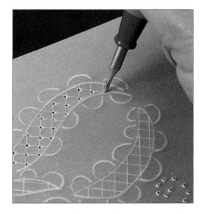

1. Working on the back of the parchment and using a ruler with a grid and the perforating tool, emboss parallel lines across the ribbon. Do not press too hard.

2. Turn the parchment round and starting in the middle, cross hatch with lines at right angles to the first lines. The grid on the ruler will help.

3. Place the parchment, right side up on the perforating mat and use the perforating tool to make holes where the lines cross.

4. Turn the parchment over. Using the embossing tool, rub each of the half moons with a back and forth motion.

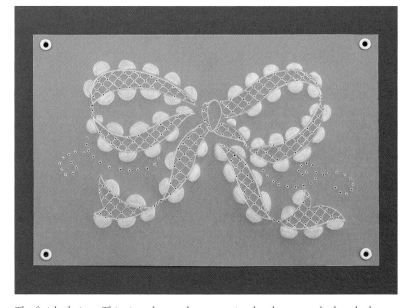

The finished piece. This time the parchment project has been attached to the base card using eyelets. Parchment work shows to better advantage on a dark background like this.

Colouring parchment

Sometimes you may want to use coloured parchment or add colour to areas of the design to give a different effect to your work. Here are some methods that I use.

Using inkpads

The ink from dye inkpads dries fairly quickly, and is easily applied to the back of the parchment using a cosmetic sponge. You can make the colour paler by wiping off excess ink. Check what the colours look like from the right side of the work.

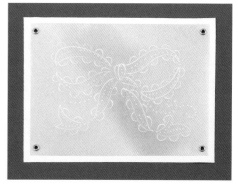

1. Place the parchment face down on a scrap of card. Using a cosmetic sponge, dab on blue ink. Any excess ink can be wiped off using a clean sponge.

2. Dab on red ink using a fresh sponge. It is a good idea to label your sponges with the ink colour so that you do not mix them up!

The finished card. I have added a third colour, then mounted the project on to a pale coloured layer, which shows the coloured parchment better, and attached it to the base card using eyelets.

Spot colouring

This is another easy way of adding a little colour. I use permanent markers as they dry quickly. The colour is applied to the back of the project so remember to check the appearance from the front, which will be different.

1. Place the parchment face down. Using a pale blue permanent marker, colour some of the ribbon.

2. Add dark blue and before the ink dries, blend the colours together using a flat no. 4 paint brush.

The finished card is attached to a dark, toning coloured base card using eyelets.

Colouring with pencils

Adding colour to your projects using coloured pencils is the method favoured in South America and some delightful effects can be achieved quite simply. Apply light strokes of the pencil to the back of the parchment, starting with the palest and moving on to darker colours. Check the appearance from the front. Any excess colour can be removed with a plastic eraser. After that you can use the blender pencil to blend colours. This does tend to make colours slightly darker.

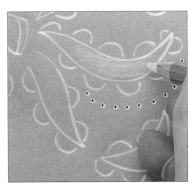

1. Use a pale blue coloured pencil first.

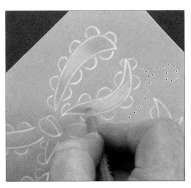

2. Then use a dark blue pencil, overlapping the pale blue slightly.

Tip

You can always rub out mistakes with a plastic eraser.

3. Use a blender pencil over the whole area to smooth out the pencil marks.

4. On the hard embossing mat, use the large estralina on the back of the parchment to make a circle in each half-moon.

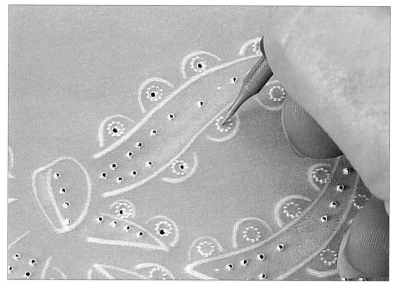

5. Lay the parchment, wrong side up, on to stencil 3 and pierce the pattern in the ribbons using the perforating tool.

6. Turn the parchment the right side up and pierce a hole in the middle of each estralina circle.

The finished card

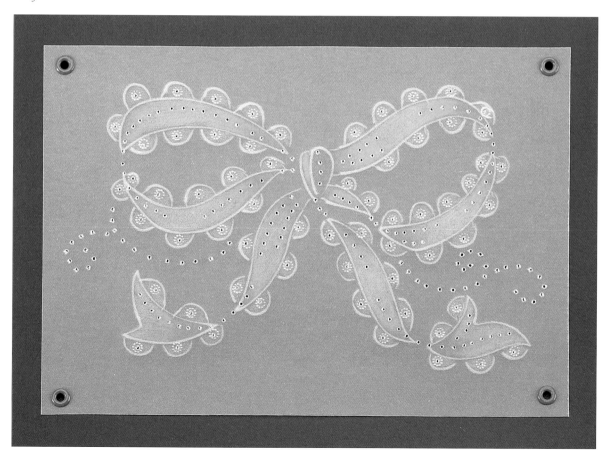

Bonny Bonnet

This project shows you how you can turn a stencil in order to alter the layout of the design. The stencil has also been reversed so that the bonnet faces a different way. If you are reversing a design, I would recommend that you turn all three stencils before you begin to avoid any problems. By altering the layout of the work in this way, space for a greeting has been created to the right of the ribbons. Spot colouring is used and you are shown how to use an estralina (a Brazilian decorative embossing tool) and also a perforating grid to make the Argentinian style decorative perforating on the hat itself.

You will need

Basic kit and Bonnet
three-step stencil

Large and small estralinas

Fun foam mat

South American style hard
embossing mat

Dual-tip medium/small ball
embossing tool

A5 parchment paper

A4 green card

Perforating grid (see page 9)

Permanent marker and
cotton bud

Low tack tape and index tabs

Masking tape

Medium circle hand punch

Eyelet kit

Six green eyelets

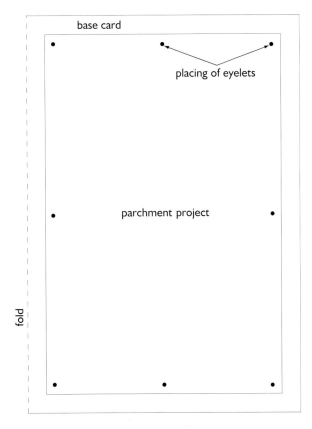

base card

placing of eyelets

parchment project

fold

The pattern for the card, shown half of actual size. Enlarge it to full size on a photocopier.

The control piece

1. Secure the parchment to the Mini Shapeboss base. Reverse stencil 1 and secure it on top, using the pegs on the left-hand side only. The top of the parchment should line up with the top of the stencil, and the right-hand side with the right-hand side of the stencil as shown.

2. Turn the kit base around so you can work comfortably. Using the medium ball embossing tool, emboss the hat and chin bow.

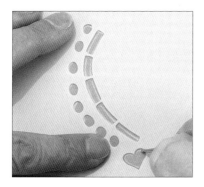

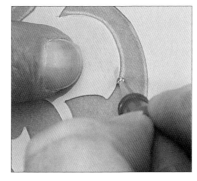

3. Secure stencil 2 and emboss the top and bottom lines of the hat band and the heart.

4. Attach stencil 3 and emboss the lines of the hat only – do not do any perforating.

5. Place stencil 1 on the embossing mat and turn the stencil so that the ribbons flow downwards rather than sideways. Lay the parchment over it and emboss the top part of the ribbons.

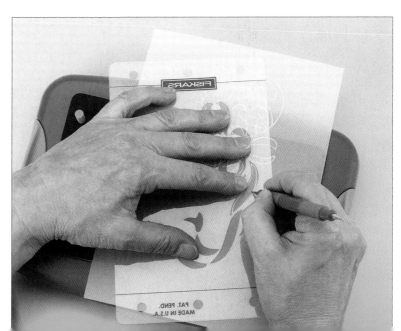

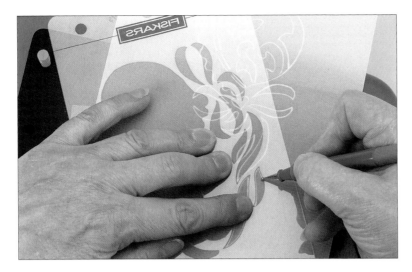

6. Keeping the parchment in place, turn the stencil slightly again so that the second part of the ribbons flows downwards in the same direction as the top part rather than at an angle. Emboss the second part.

7. Turn the stencil a third time so that the lower ends of the ribbon flow across. Emboss.

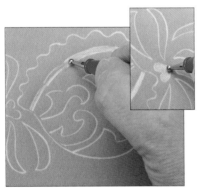

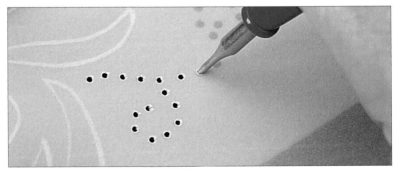

8. Place the parchment face down on the embossing mat and with the large embossing tool emboss the hat band. Then emboss the heart at the top of the ribbons.

9. Place the perforating stencil on to the fun foam mat and lay the project over it. You will be able to see the perforating holes through the paper. Checking the control piece, position the parchment correctly and perforate the swirls near the bow, then move the paper again and perforate by the ends of the ribbons.

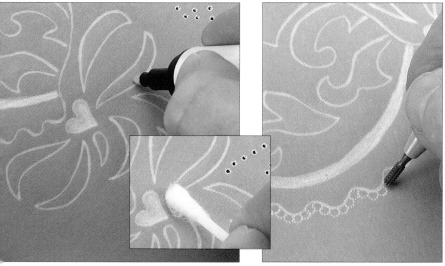

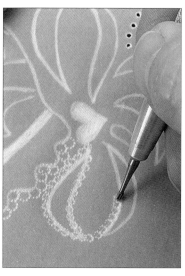

10. Turn the parchment over and spot colour the reverse side of the ribbons using permanent marker. You can wipe off any mistakes with a cotton bud.

11. Lay the work on the hard embossing mat and use the large estralina to decorate around the brim of the hat.

12. With the small estralina, decorate the edges of the ribbons.

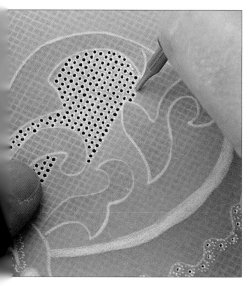

13. Place the perforating grid on the base, over the mat. Secure the project on top using small pieces of masking tape. Perforate every hole in the uncoloured and non-embossed areas of the hat and brim.

14. Trim the parchment to measure 12.3 x 19.4cm (4$^7/_8$ x 7$^5/_8$in). Tape your parchment to the full-sized photocopy of the pattern on page 16 using index tabs. Use a medium circle hand punch to make six holes for the eyelets as shown.

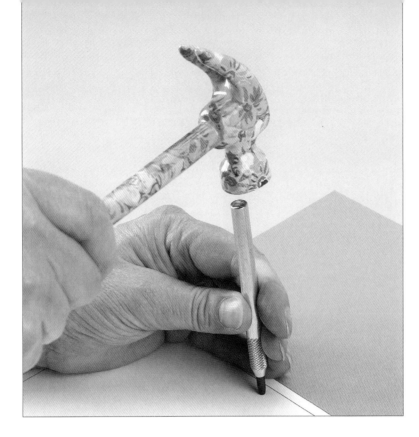

15. Fold the A4 green card in half and trim it to measure 13.3 x 20.4cm (5¼ x 8in) folded. Open the card. Attach the photocopied pattern to the front of the opened card and place over the eyelet setting mat. Place the eyelet piercing tool over one of the holes on the pattern and give the tool a sharp tap with the hammer.

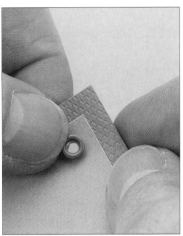

16. Repeat for all the eyelet holes, then attach the parchment to the card using six eyelets.

17. Turn the card over, place the setting tool in each eyelet and tap it with the hammer as before. This secures the eyelets.

The finished card. The base card and the eyelets are almost the same colour as the permanent marker used to colour the parchment. There is room for you to add a craft sticker greeting between the hanging ribbons and the right-hand edge of the parchment.

Here are some different ideas for you to try out.

Top left: The stencil has been reversed and cross hatching has been used in the main areas of the bonnet, whilst on the shaped areas and some of the ribbons the stippling technique has been used. The corners of the base card have been shaped with corner rounder scissors.

Bottom left: The stencil has been used the right way round and white pencil has been used on the back to shade in areas of the ribbons and the bonnet. A piece of patterned vellum in virtually the same colour as the base card has been used as a layer and a photo corner punch has been used to mount the parchment on to it. The layer has then been mounted on to the base card using spray adhesive.

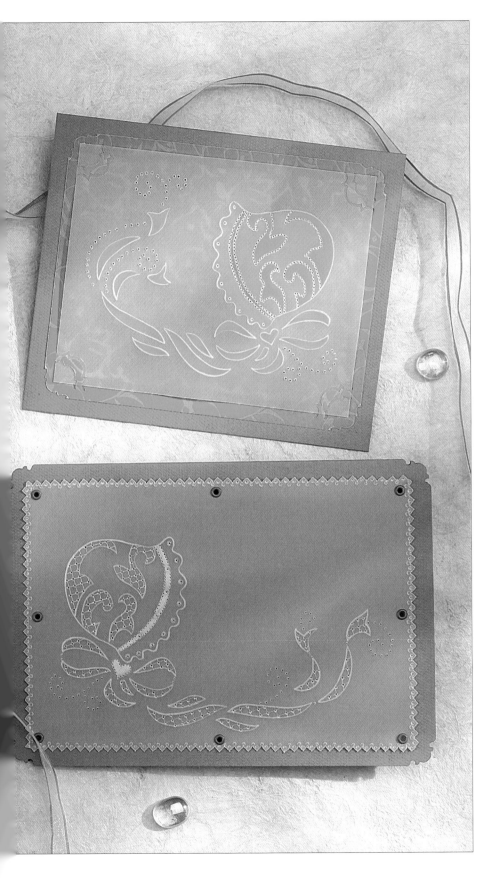

Top right: Here again the stencil has been used the right way round but this time the hat and ribbons have been coloured using coloured pencil.

Bottom right: The stencil has been reversed and the ribbons have been extended in a similar way to those of the main project. The shapes on the hat have been cross hatched and the small estralina has been used where the lines cross over and on the hat brim. A Puerto Rican chevron cutting tool has been used round the edges of the parchment and this has then been decorated using a small estralina.

Snowflakes

Some parchment projects lend themselves to mounting in aperture cards. For this card I have used a circle cutter to make an aperture in the front of the card, and a 'neatener' to tidy up the inside of the card, behind the aperture where the parchment project is displayed.

You will need

Basic kit and Snowflake three-step stencil

Dual-tip medium/small ball embossing tool

Circle aperture cutter

Corner rounder scissors

Large and small estralinas

South American style hard embossing mat

A4 and A5 dark blue card

A5 parchment paper

Double-sided tape

Glitter appliqué glue and cocktail stick

Snowflake craft punch

Super non-spray adhesive and tweezers

Low tack tape

White pencil

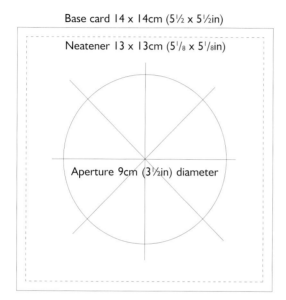

Base card 14 x 14cm (5½ x 5½in)

Neatener 13 x 13cm (5⅛ x 5⅛in)

Aperture 9cm (3½in) diameter

The pattern for the card shown half size. Enlarge it on a photocopier.

1. Cut the parchment to 10 x 10cm (4 x 4in) and make a white pencil cross in the centre. Place stencil 1 on the base with the pegs on the left-hand side, and align the white pencil cross with the centre of the large snowflake stencil. Secure the parchment to the pad using low tack tape.

2. Using the medium tool, emboss the large snowflake.

3. Change to stencil 3 and emboss the inner snowflake. Stencil 2 is not used in this project.

4. Using the perforating tool, perforate around the outer design.

5. Place the project on the hard embossing mat and fill in the central shape using the large estralina.

6. Also using the large estralina, add shapes between the diamonds.

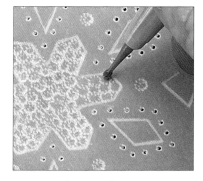

7. Use the small estralina in the centre of the large estralina shapes in the snowflake.

8. Fill in the outer shapes using the small estralina.

9. Make a dot at the tip of each of the diamonds and outer shapes with the small estralina.

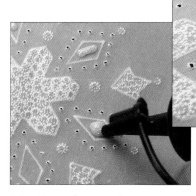

10. Turn the parchment over and on the right side place a dot of glitter appliqué glue in each of the diamonds. Use a cocktail stick to spread the glue to the edges.

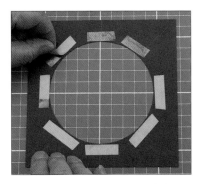

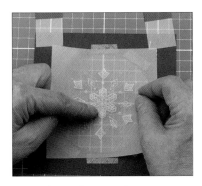

11. Fold the A4 card in half and cut to measure 14 x 14cm (5½ x 5½in). Mark the centre of the inside front with a white pencil. Set the aperture cutter to 9cm (3½in) diameter, place the needle over the centre mark and turn the cutter. Repeat with a 13 x 13cm (5⅛ x 5⅛in) square cut from A5 card to make a neatener.

12. Place pieces of double-sided tape around the aperture in the neatener. Peel off the backing.

13. Place the parchment right side up centrally over the aperture in the neatener and press on to the tape.

14. Attach the neatener to the inside front of the card using double-sided tape so that the project is displayed through the aperture.

15. Round off the corners of the card using corner rounder scissors.

16. Punch twelve small parchment snowflakes. Using a pair of tweezers, place the snowflakes on to a strip of super non-spray adhesive.

17. Peel off the snowflakes and place them on the corners of the card to finish it.

*When the card stands on the mantelpiece, the light will enhance the translucent
parchment and glitter, giving it a frosty look.*

Top: This card uses the other large snowflake on the stencil and half of the small one on each side. Stippling techniques have been used and the lines extending from the main snowflake were embossed using a ruler and perforating tool. Large and small estralinas were used to decorate the ends of the lines and the snowflake. A photo corner punch was used on the layer and the parchment was slotted into the holes. The layer was then mounted on to a white base card using spray adhesive.

Left: The same snowflake used in the main project features again here. Decoration is created by small and large estralinas and also embossed lines. The project is layered on to deep blue metallic paper, then on to gold paper, and all the layers are attached to the base card using eyelets.

Roses are Red

In this project you will see how to use a Puerto Rican cutting tool to make a scalloped edge. This project also shows you how to sew the parchment project on to a card using metallic thread, and how to incorporate beads. Only part of the stencil has been used.

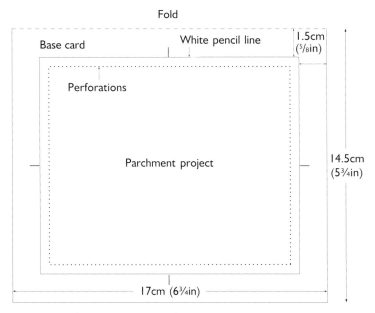

The pattern for the card shown half size, with measurements marked full size. Enlarge on a photocopier.

You will need

Basic kit and Rose three-step stencil

Dual-tip medium/small ball embossing tool

Large and small estralinas

Puerto Rican scallop cutting tool

Fun foam mat

South American style hard embossing mat

A5 parchment paper

Coloured pencils: three shades of red and three shades of green

White pencil and plastic eraser

A4 and A5 red card

Gold metallic thread and needle

Double-sided tape

Low tack tape

1. Place stencil 1 on the base with the trade name to the left and the pegs on the right. Secure the parchment to the mat using low tack tape. Emboss the rose design and some of the leaves using the medium embossing tool.

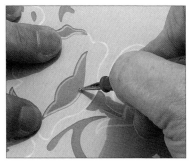

2. Emboss stencil 2 in the same way.

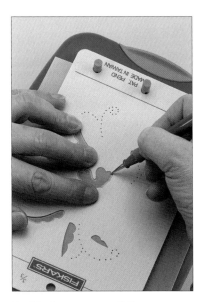

3. Emboss stencil 3.

30

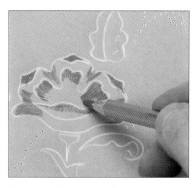

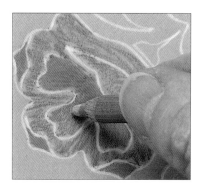

4. Place stencil 3 on the fun foam mat, lay the parchment on top and perforate the curlicues in the correct areas.

5. Use the pencils to colour the rose on the back of the parchment: the palest shades first, then the mid-tones.

6. Apply the darkest shade of red, then use the blender pencil to merge the colours.

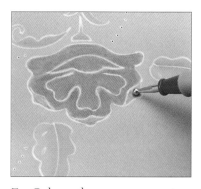

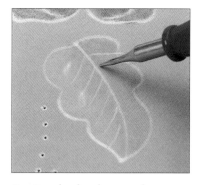

7. Colour the green areas in the same way. Still working on the back of the parchment, emboss the petal tips using the large ball tool so that they turn pale pink.

8. Working on the right side of the parchment, emboss the tops of the inner petals.

9. On the back, use the perforating tool to draw the veins of the leaves.

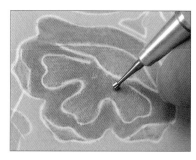

10. Also on the back, use the small estralina to emboss the flower anthers.

11. Place the work right side up on the fun foam mat and perforate along the central vein of the leaf using the perforating tool.

12. Place the parchment right side up on the full-sized pattern. Draw in the white pencil line as marked and pierce along the perforations to create a sewing line.

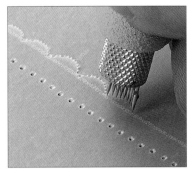

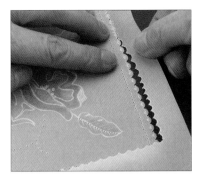

13. Lay the parchment right side up on the fun foam mat and use the Puerto Rican cutting tool to cut scalloped edges, lining up the two outermost needles with the white line. Rub out the white line using a plastic eraser.

14. Lay the work on the hard embossing mat, wrong side up. Use the large estralina along the scalloped edges as shown.

15. Carefully pull the edges away from the finished parchment project, tearing along the scalloped edge.

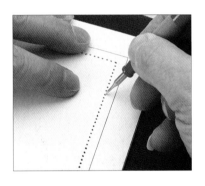

16. Fold the A4 red card in half and lay it on the pattern, matching the fold to the fold line on the pattern. Cut this base card to size (see page 30). Perforate the sewing line again, using the same holes you pierced on the parchment.

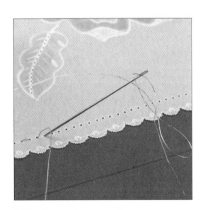

17. Sew the parchment to the card using gold metallic thread. Secure the start and end of the thread to the inside front of the card using double-sided tape.

18. To make the neatener, cut a rectangle 12.5 x 15.3cm (5 x 6in) from A5 card. Use double-sided tape to attach it to the inside front of the card to hide the stitching on the back.

The finished card has an elegant simplicity. A craft sticker greeting can be added on the lower left-hand side of the rose.

The stencil has been reversed to create the top rose, whilst the lower one uses it the right way round. The roses have been coloured using various shades of yellow and the edges were cut using a Puerto Rican chevron cutting tool and decorated using an estralina. The project was sewn on to the base card using gold metallic thread.

Top: The red rose has been mounted in an aperture card as shown in the Snowflakes project. Centre: Embossing, the perforating grid and white pencil have been used for a simple but striking effect. Bottom: This example uses the whole of the template. Embossing and perforating techniques have been used without further decoration.

Heartfelt Wishes

Heart motifs can be used for many occasions as well as Valentine's Day. This project is an unusual way of sending a special photograph to family and friends. I scanned the area of the photograph I wanted and printed it the right size, 3.5 x 3.7cm (1⅜ x 1½in) to fit behind the central heart. A double heart project could hold the photographs of an engaged couple, the bride and groom or even an anniversary couple.

You will need

Basic kit and the Hearts three-step stencil

Dual-tip medium/small ball embossing tool

Large and small estralinas

Puerto Rican straight edge cutting tool

Fun foam mat

South American style hard embossing mat

Ruler with a grid

Perforating grid

Photo corner punch

A5 parchment paper

A4 off-white card

A5 blue paper

Double-sided tape, low tack tape and index tabs

White pencil and plastic eraser

Fold

Base card

Layer

Parchment project

Placement lines

The pattern for the card shown half size. Enlarge it on a photocopier.

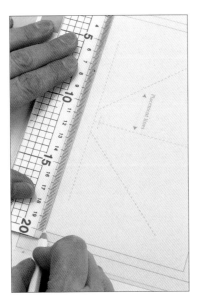

1. Tape the parchment on top of the photocopied, full-size pattern. Using a white pencil, draw the placement lines and the outside edge of the parchment project. Cut the parchment to size along the white lines.

2. Tape the parchment to the fun foam mat. Secure stencil 1 on top, lining up the large heart with the central placement line on the parchment. Emboss the heart.

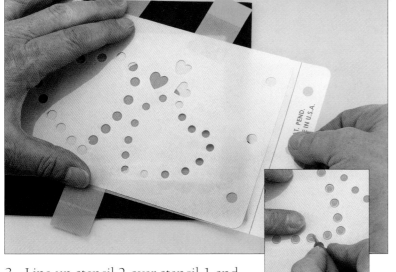

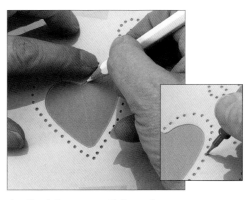

3. Line up stencil 2 over stencil 1 and tape it in place. Pull stencil 1 out from underneath. Emboss the circles.

4. Position stencil 3 and remove stencil 2 in the same way. Use a white pencil to draw around the heart, then perforate the dots.

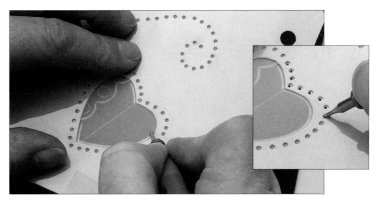

5. Line up the small heart on stencil 1 with one of the placement lines at the side and emboss it.

6. Secure stencil 3 in the same way. Emboss the inside of the heart and perforate around the outside. Reverse the stencils and repeat steps 5 and 6 for the small heart on the other side. Erase the white lines.

7. Use a large estralina to decorate the outer circles of the large heart and between its perforations, then the edges of the smaller hearts. Use the small estralina between the perforations in the smaller hearts, inside the large estralina shapes and at the points of all the scalloped edges.

8. Using a perforating tool and a ruler with a grid, cross hatch around the centre of the large heart, as shown on page 12.

9. Use the small estralina to decorate the points at which the lines cross.

10. Secure the perforating grid over the perforating mat on the base and tape the parchment, right side up, to the grid. Perforate the centres of the side hearts.

11. With the parchment wrong side up, use stencil 3 to perforate curlicues above each side heart.

12. Cut the blue paper to 18.7 x 11.2cm (7^3/$_8$ x 4^3/$_8$in). Punch each corner with the photo corner punch.

13. Fix the parchment to the blue paper layer by slipping its corners into the punched photo corners. Secure it in place by applying double-sided tape to the back of blue layer as shown.

14. Place the work on the fun foam mat and use the Puerto Rican straight edge cutting tool to cut out the large heart, cutting through the blue paper as well as the parchment.

Tip

It is easier to line up the corner pattern if you use the punch upside down.

15. Attach index tabs to the back of your chosen photograph as shown.

16. Position your photograph carefully in the heart-shaped aperture.

17. Secure the photograph at the back using double-sided tape, and remove the index tabs. Cut the off-white card to 26.6 x 20.6cm (10½ x 8⅛in) and fold. Peel the backing off all the double-sided tape and mount the blue layer and project on the folded card.

The finished card. You could also cut out the centres of the small hearts if you want to include more photographs.

The parchment project has been attached to the card using eyelets, and then the
centre of the heart has been perforated to create an aperture. If you wish, a suitable
greeting can be added to the inside so that it shows through the aperture.

Top: The two smaller hearts have been used and a hole punch from the eyelet kit has been used in the scalloped outline. Decorative perforating has been used in both heart centres.
Bottom: The large heart has been used twice, once the right way round and then with the stencil reversed to produced this overlapped hearts design.

Beautiful Butterfly

Butterflies are always popular subjects for card makers as they come in all different sizes, shapes and colours. Parchment gives you an even wider range of ways you can depict them and use them in your card making.

You will need

Basic kit and the Butterfly three-step stencil

Dual-tip medium/small ball embossing tool

White pencil

Large and small estralinas

Fun foam mat

South American style hard embossing mat

Perforating grid (see page 9)

A5 parchment paper

Permanent markers in three colours of your choice

Ruler with a grid

Medium circle hand punch

A4 off-white card

Dark blue metallic paper, 12 x 12.5cm (4¾ x 5in)

Four blue eyelets

Eyelet kit

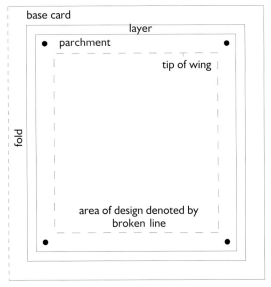

The pattern for the Beautiful Butterfly card, shown half size. Enlarge it on a photocopier.

1. Photocopy the pattern. Cut the parchment to 11 x 11.5cm (4⅜ x 4½in). Using the photocopied pattern as a guide, punch four holes with the circle hand punch.

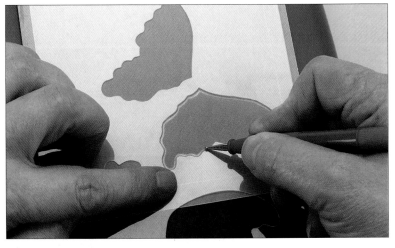

2. Position the parchment under stencil 1. Emboss with the medium embossing tool.

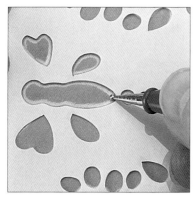

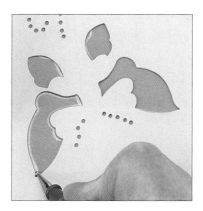

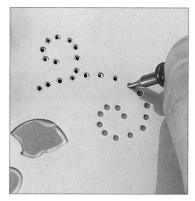

3. Change to stencil 2 and emboss the body and the four shapes beside it.

4. Using stencil 3, emboss the wing shapes.

5. Working on the fun foam mat, use the same stencil and the perforating tool to pierce the curlicues.

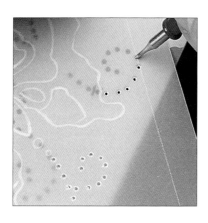

6. Move the parchment and position it over the same stencil to add extra pierced curlicues to each side of the wings.

7. Working on the back of the parchment, colour in areas of the butterfly using three different permanent markers.

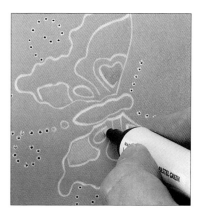

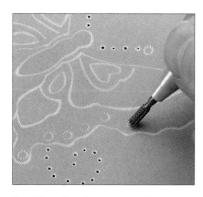

8. Use the large estralina to make circles along the inside edges of the wings, and add one at the tip of each antenna, one just below the body and four in a row along the body.

9. Use the small estralina inside the large estralina circles at the tip of each antenna, and along the body. Add a small circle below the large circle beyond the end of the body.

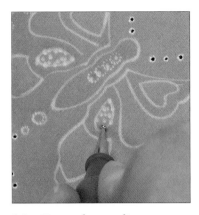  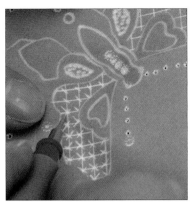

10. Using the medium embossing tool, add dots to the tear shapes on the wings, and at the centres of the estralina circles at the edges of the wings and along the body.

11. Cross hatch the area shown using the perforating tool and a ruler with a grid.

12. Use the perforating tool to make freehand crosses where the cross hatched lines intersect. Press down gently.

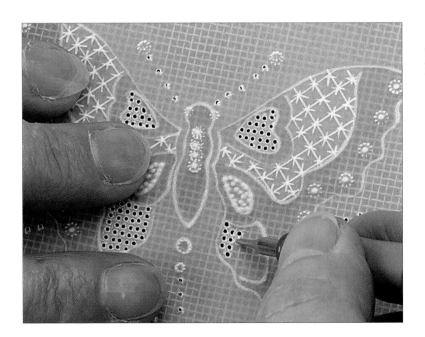

13. Secure the parchment over the perforating grid and perforate the areas shown.

Opposite

The finished Beautiful Butterfly card. Use the pattern, enlarged on a photocopier to full size, as a guide to punch the eyelet holes in the parchment and the dark blue paper layer. Cut the off-white card to 28 x 14.5cm (11 x 5¾in) and fold it in half. Punch eyelet holes in the front of the card only. Using the eyelet kit and four blue eyelets, secure the parchment and blue layer to the card.

*The all-white effects give this uncoloured parchment a lacy look, and the design,
with its row of smaller butterflies on one side has a slightly oriental feel to it.*

Top: Some areas of the wings have been coloured using permanent marker, and the Puerto Rican straight edge cutting tool has been used round the outside edges of the wings so that they can be raised slightly after the project has been mounted. The Puerto Rican scallop cutting tool adds a decorative edge to the parchment.
Bottom: The large butterflies have been created by using the stencil and then reversing it. The edges of the small butterflies' wings have been perforated to give them a slightly raised appearance.

Index